THE POWER OF
FORGIVENESS

The Glory of Christianity is to Conquer by Forgiveness

Apostle Rudolph S. Johnson Sr.

THE GLORY CLOUD PUBLICATIONS LLC

Copyright © 2009 by Rudolph S. Johnson Sr.

All rights reserved. No part of this publication may be reproduced, distributed or transmitted in any form or by any means, including photocopying, recording, or other electronic or mechanical methods, without the prior written permission of the publisher, except in the case of brief quotations embodied in critical reviews and certain other noncommercial uses permitted by copyright law. For permission requests, write to the publisher, addressed "Attention: Permissions Coordinator," at the address below.

Rudolph Johnson/ Restoration World Ministries
PO Box 35 Street Address
Belcamp MD 21017
www.rwministries.net

Publisher's Note: This is a work of fiction. Names, characters, places, and incidents are a product of the author's imagination. Locales and public names are sometimes used for atmospheric purposes. Any resemblance to actual people, living or dead, or to businesses, companies, events, institutions, or locales is completely coincidental.

Book Layout ©2017 BookDesignTemplates.com

Ordering Information:
Quantity sales. Special discounts are available on quantity purchases by corporations, associations, and others. For details, contact the "Special Sales Department" at the address above.

The Power of Forgiveness / Rudolph S. Johnson Sr. – 2nd ed.
ISBN 978-0-9889866-9-5

Contents

Dedication..
Acknowledgements.......................................
Introduction 1
1 Let's Make It Personal 3
2 Scripture Reading Impartation......................... 7
3 Give Forgiveness.. 13
4 No Condemnation 15
5 In the Morning 17
6 Can I Forgive?.. 19
7 Unforgiveness 21
8 Blessing on Forgiveness 23
9 Power of Forgiveness 25
10 Will Versus Consciousness............................... 27
11 Give to Forgive 31
ABOUT THE AUTHOR 33

Apostle Rudolph S. Johnson Sr.

Dedication

I bring peace and blessings to all who read this prophetic realization through the Holy Spirit. It is my heart's desire that we as believers understand that forgiveness is a principle that the Body of Christ must exemplify.

The name of my ministry is Restoration World Ministries, Inc. *Restoration is defined as getting back life that has been lost or even given away. It's defined as what has challenged us through everyday mishaps. As you turn through the pages, I am encouraging you as the reader to find Restoration in giving to forgive. I believe that we not only need to give finances, clothes and jewelry, but we need to give forgiveness so that we as brothers and sisters can live in harmony and peace. Give forgiveness and love, continue the pattern of your actions and watch God do great and marvelous things for you.*

Enjoy this reading and partake of the heavenly blessing as you become obedient to forgive. When you truly forgive, Restoration has finally come! Blessings to you, my beloved brothers and sisters.

Apostle Rudolph S. Johnson Sr.

Acknowledgements

I want to thank my loving wife, *Prophetess Fern. W. Johnson*, my daughters, *Theressa, Sondeania* and *Rudina*, and my son, *Rudolph S. Johnson, Jr.* for their support and prayers. Thanks also to my *Restoration* family, *Prophetess Carmen Crockson* and those who have encouraged me to impact the kingdom of God with divine words of wisdom.

The power of forgiveness is the power of releasing your thoughts over to the power of God, accepting the freedom to be free in your spirit
—*The Power of Forgiveness*

Introduction

In Psalm 51, David had four requests after he had been with Bath-Sheba. His request was that God would forgive him.

His first request: Have mercy upon me, O God, according unto the multitude of they tender mercies.

His second request: Blot out my transgressions.

His third request: Wash me thoroughly from mine iniquity.

His fourth request: Cleanse me from my sin.

When asking forgiveness, we become a man or woman after God's own heart, regardless of what we've done. And as the Father forgives us, we should also forgive others. Then we all can do like David did in Psalm 51:10-12:

RUDOLPH S. JOHNSON SR.

"Create in me a clean heart, O God, and renew a right spirit within me, cast me not away from the presence; and take not thy Holy Spirit from me. Restore unto me the joy of thy salvation and uphold me with thy free spirit.

That's the place we want to get to- Restoration.

1 Let's Make It Personal

My experience with forgiveness was a process and it will be one with all of you. Forgiveness must first be a lifestyle of practice and a mind determined to be active in this area. Forgiveness comes from the heart. It is articulated out of your mouth and tells your brain that you are capable and willing to forgive. But you will never know when you're in a period in your life where you need to follow your actions up with forgiving. So be truthful when you read this book. Yes, I too have been hurt by so-called friends, church members, pastors, leaders, and a variety of people. And yes, it's painful. Even now, I've felt the urge to get back at them because of what they have done to me in the past. However, I've learned over the course of time that I must make a conscious decision in my heart to forgive all the pain and disappointment that has come my way.

My experience in forgiving is the knowledge that it does me no good not to forgive. Being unforgiving causes me to have an unbalanced life with myself and my savior. It also keeps me from looking my adversary in the eye. I was at a point in my life where I did not want to forgive and wanted revenge. But then, I started reading more about what Yahshua went through and I took greater examination of myself. As a Christian, I told myself I would forgive everything and everyone who was out to hurt me, damage me, or put me down. It was not so much about me but rather what I stood for. That was the Christ that lives in me. Now, I want you to know it takes daily practice to learn to forgive. It can't be done with just words but it must also be proven by acting upon what you say. You will never know if you can forgive until you are put in a position where it is not comfortable for you to forgive.

I wanted the ones who hurt me, lied to me, didn't trust me, stabbed me in my back and gave me a Judas kiss to see the Christ in me. This is one of the reasons why I'm able to forgive. Another is it's not the person but what's working in the inside of them that's contrary to the truth of the Holy Spirit. I wanted to see beyond their faults and see their needs; this is another way I can find forgiveness. My love for them is in helping them when they need it. Love always passes and looks beyond what had happened and focuses on the power of forgiveness.

Forgiveness generates a bigger God inside of me that I can't explain. When I think about all the things I've done in the past and how Christ still forgave me, I realize I must be that personal instrument that will make a melody in someone's heart to see forgiving is possible at all levels of our lives. Prayer and daily confession allowed me to see myself in situations that would allow me to forgive. I'm always aware that the flesh and the Spirit are at odds with one another. I've decided in my mind and heart that when the flesh wants to dominate me, I will ask God to forgive me and allow the Holy Spirit to take precedence in my life. I allow the energy that's inside of me to let others know forgiveness is real and it can take place if we would make it one of our daily confessions. I believe that to forgive is to love and to love is to forgive. Living a life of forgiveness will bring peace to you as you and I continue to encounter negative points in our lives.

In my experience, I've realized it takes time to forgive. It does not happen overnight. It's not as if you go to bed and wake up the next morning and you've forgiven everyone who hurt you—no! You must decide to do what you need to do to influence the one you've had problems with. I'm not saying you should forget the situation or problems that occur. I am saying, however, that when you encounter that person, there is nothing in your heart. I needed to see if I was being true to myself by helping or doing whatever it took to help the one who hurt me, lied to me, or even tried to disgrace my name. You will know because you will focus on forgiving more than not forgiving. When I can do that I feel good about myself and that person becomes overwhelmed by how I treat them with love and respect. It is as if nothing ever happened. When you get to that point in your life, you can truly say restoration is in order.

When you truly forgive them from your heart, there is a transformation and restoration that takes place. I believe the order of your life is understanding forgiveness, which is what Christ did for us. He forgave us so we could live a life that leads to a place of restoration.

RUDOLPH S. JOHNSON SR.

2 Scripture Reading Impartation

Luke 7:36-50: *And one of the Pharisees desired him that he would eat with him. And he went into the Pharisee's house, and sat down to meat. And, behold, a woman in the city, which was a sinner, when she knew that Jesus sat at meat in the Pharisee's house, brought an alabaster box of ointment, and stood at his feet behind him weeping, and began to wash his feet with tears, and did wipe them with the hairs of her head, and kissed his feet, and anointed them with the ointment. Now when the Pharisee which had bidden him saw it, he spake within himself, saying, This man, if he were a prophet, would have known who and what manner of woman this is that toucheth him: for she is a sinner. And Jesus answering said unto him, Simon, I have somewhat to say unto thee. And he saith, Master, say on. There was a certain creditor which had two debtors: the one owed five hundred pence, and the other fifty. And when they had nothing to pay, he frankly forgave them both. Tell me therefore, which of them will love him most? Simon answered and said, I suppose that he, to whom he forgave most. And he said unto him, Thou hast rightly judged. And he turned to the woman, and said unto Simon, Seest thou this woman? I entered into thine house, thou gavest me no water for my feet: but she hath washed my feet with tears, and wiped them with the hairs of her head. Thou gavest me no kiss: but this woman since the time I came in hath not ceased to kiss my feet. My head with oil thou didst not anoint: but this woman hath anointed my feet with ointment. Wherefore I say unto thee, Her sins, which are many, are forgiven; for she loved much: but to whom little is forgiven, the same loveth little. And he said unto her, Thy sins are forgiven. And they that sat at meat with him began to say within themselves, Who is this that forgiveth sins also? And he said to the woman, Thy faith hath saved thee; go in peace.*

God will forgive you as you have forgiven others.

Luke 11:1: *And it came to pass, that, as he was praying in a certain place, when he ceased, one of his disciples said unto him, Lord, teach us to pray, as John also taught his disciples.*

Witness the power of forgiveness.

Luke 15:11-31: *And he said, A certain man had two sons: and the younger of them said to his father, Father, give me the portion of goods that falleth to me. And he divided unto them his living. And not many days after the younger son gathered all together, and took his journey into a far country, and there wasted his substance with riotous living. And when he had spent all, there arose a mighty famine in that land; and he began to be in want. And he went and joined himself to a citizen of that country; and he sent him into his fields to feed swine. And he would fain have filled his belly with the husks that the swine did eat: and no man gave unto him. And when he came to himself, he said, How many hired servants of my father's have bread enough and to spare, and I perish with hunger! I will arise and go to my father, and will say unto him, Father, I have sinned against heaven, and before thee, and am no more worthy to be called thy son: make me as one of thy hired servants. And he arose, and came to his father. But when he was yet a great way off, his father saw him, and had compassion, and ran, and fell on his neck, and kissed him. And the son said unto him, Father, I have sinned against heaven, and in thy sight, and am no more worthy to be called thy son. But the father said to his servants, Bring forth the best robe, and put it on him; and put a ring on his hand, and shoes on his feet: and bring hither the fatted calf, and kill it; and let us eat, and be merry: for this my son was dead, and is alive again; he was lost, and is found. And they began to be merry. Now his elder son was in the field: and as he came and drew nigh to the house, he heard music and dancing. And he called one of the servants, and asked what these things meant. [27] And he said unto him, Thy brother is come; and thy father hath killed the fatted calf, because he hath received him safe and sound. [28] And he was angry, and would not go in: therefore came his father out, and intreated him. [29] And he answering said to his father, Lo, these many years do I serve thee, neither transgressed I at any time thy commandment: and yet thou never gavest me a kid, that I might make merry with my friends: [30] but as soon as this thy son was come, which hath devoured thy living with harlots, thou hast killed for him the fatted calf. [31] And he said unto him, Son, thou art ever with me, and all that I have is thine.*

If we confess our sins, he will forgive and cleanse us.

1 John 1:8: *If we say that we have no sin, we deceive ourselves and the truth is not in us.*

1 John 2:11: *But he that hateth his brother is in darkness and walketh in darkness, and knoweth not whither he goeth, be cause that darkness hath blinded his eyes.*

Love and forgive your enemies.

Luke 6:27-38: *But I say unto you which hear, Love your enemies, do good to them which hate you, bless them that curse you, and pray for them which despitefully use you. And unto him that smiteth thee on the one cheek offer also the other; and him that taketh away thy cloke forbid not to take thy coat also. Give to every man that asketh of thee; and of him that taketh away thy goods ask them not again. And as ye would that men should do to you, do ye also to them likewise. For if ye love them which love you, what thank have ye? for sinners also love those that love them. And if ye do good to them which do good to you, what thank have ye? for sinners also do even the same. And if ye lend to them of whom ye hope to receive, what thank have ye? for sinners also lend to sinners, to receive as much again. But love ye your enemies, and do good, and lend, hoping for nothing again; and your reward shall be great, and ye shall be the children of the Highest: for he is kind unto the unthankful and to the evil. Be ye therefore merciful, as your Father also is merciful. Judge not, and ye shall not be judged: condemn not, and ye shall not be condemned: forgive, and ye shall be forgiven: give, and it shall be given unto you; good measure, pressed down, and shaken together, and running over, shall men give into your bosom. For with the same measure that ye mete withal it shall be measured to you again.*

Do not let anything hinder your prayer; forgive so that you may be forgiven.

Mark 11:24-25: *Therefore I say unto you, What things soever ye desire, when ye pray, believe that ye receive them, and ye shall have them. And when ye stand praying, forgive, if ye have ought against any: that your Father also which is in heaven may forgive you your trespasses.*

Let's get personal. All scriptures are available for your spiritual growth. It's all real and true. We must follow the principles and examples that are in the Word of God; if not, you will hold bitterness in your heart. The latter makes your own words show feelings of intense animosity, resentment, or vindictiveness. In other words, allowing yourself to be unforgiving is something you don't want. Don't carry bitterness, envy or strife in your heart. Instead, replace it with love, kindness, and most of all, forgiveness. Can you do it? Yes, you can. If we start applying the scripture to our daily walk, you can see a change in yourself. You can do it! Just apply the Word to your situation and a brand-new you will be walking the Earth representing Jesus Christ in the power of forgiveness.

Colossians 3:13: *Forbearing one another, and forgiving one another; if any man have a quarrel against any: even as Christ forgave you, so also do ye.*

Philippians 3:13: *Brethren, I count not myself to have apprehended: but this one thing I do, forgetting those things which are behind, and reaching forth unto those things which are before.*

Romans 12:2: *And be not conformed to this world: but be ye transformed by the renewing of your mind, that ye may prove what is that good, and acceptable, and perfect, will of God.*

Romans 8:28: *And we know that all things work together for good to them that love God, to them who are the called according to his purpose.*

The purpose for forgiveness will work for you. Let's go for it! It all works out for an extraordinary person such as you. Congratulations, you can make it over one hurdle at a time. It means you're on your way to a victorious life in Christ.

3 Give Forgiveness

In exercising the power of forgiveness, we must first understand Jesus' lifestyle and his example of the power of forgiveness. You must do so to follow the principles of forgiveness. It is a daily confession of your spirit to kill the flesh. Let your spirit man dominate what your flesh does not want to do. Walk in total forgiveness for your benefit and for others who are watching you. For example, when a person goes to a gym to work out, they go to get in shape. In doing so, they use muscles they have not used in quite a while, which makes it a little harder. There is pain and work necessary to get the desire results.

What is most important to us is what we work on to get impressive results; this is the same way we need to look at the power of forgiveness. I believe it's a lost principle in the Body of Christ and we as Christians should get back to really exercising this power. We should be able to forgive others if we are going to model ourselves after our Lord and Savior Jesus Christ. I thank God for giving me the name Restoration for my ministry because regardless of what people have done to you, there is always room for forgiveness.

Think of an empty room. You first walk in it and realize it will remain empty until you decide to furnish it. The room will become complete according to what you like. Your mind can be clear and imagine what you want your life to be like once you've taken inventory and examined yourself. Regardless of how bad your situation has been, you can begin to look around in your spiritual room and remove, replace, and redesign things. This will help you give to forgive. Redesign your pattern of life so you can give to forgive. Just like adding brand-new furniture or rearranging a room, you feel so much better. You can enjoy what you've done because you put effort and love into it. Therefore, Paul wrote to the church at Ephesus.

Ephesians 4:29-32: *Let no corrupt communication proceed out of your mouth, but that which is good to the use of the edifying, that is may minister grace unto the heavens and grieve not the Holy Spirit of God whereby ye are sealed unto the day of Redemption. Let all bitterness and wrath and anger and clamor and evil speaking, be put away from you, with all malice. And be kind to another, tender-hearted, forgiving one another even as God for Christ's sake hath forgiven you.*

4 No Condemnation

Condemnation is not to be pushed onto one who is in Christ, regardless of what they've done. At the church we have a motto, "Restoration is in order for all God's people."

Romans 8:1-5: *There is therefore now no condemnation to them which are in Christ Jesus, who walk not after the flesh, but after the Spirit. For the law of the Spirit of life in Christ Jesus hath made me free from the law of sin and death. For what the law could not do, in that it was weak through the flesh, God sending his own Son in the likeness of sinful flesh, and for sin, condemned sin in the flesh: that the righteousness of the law might be fulfilled in us, who walk not after the flesh, but after the Spirit. For they that are after the flesh do mind the things of the flesh; but they that are after the Spirit the things of the Spirit.*

The righteousness of Christ is in the redemption of the blood of Jesus. We have been redeemed to forgive through the power of God. We are the righteousness of God and we have been justified through his atoning blood. Though we did not deserve it, the power of forgiveness was in order of all God's people.

5 In the Morning

In the morning, exercise forgiveness by praying to God the Father through his son, Jesus Christ the anointed one, to make it your business to forgive. Getting up early in the morning, new mercy unto us will allow us to work out our salvation. We must be careful of how we look at someone else's fallen state, knowing we could be in the same predicament. Thus, morning devotional is very important. We should take inventory of ourselves first and only *then* can we be a model after Jesus Christ when people seem to treat you differently. Why in the morning? Because at that time of day, there's joy, peace and reflection in knowing that life is better when you can forgive. The cleansing element of prayer is turning our hearts and minds toward anything that's not like God and displaying forgiveness.

RUDOLPH S. JOHNSON SR.

6 Can I Forgive?

When someone hurts or damages us, as mature Christians our assignment is to forgive them. Forgiveness is accepting their apology and moving on in love like nothing ever happened. If we are going to be Christ-like, then we must allow our actions to speak for us by letting our light shine. If a brother or sister wrongs you, you are supposed to forgive them. Forgiveness opens pathways to your blessing. Always think about Jesus when the Roman soldiers beat him. He said, "Father, forgive them, for they know what they do. Some people just don't know what they're doing. Some do when it comes to your individual experiences, but the words that should come out your mouth and spirit as a Christian are, "I forgive them, for they know not what they do."

Matthew 18:21-22: *Then came Peter to him, and said, Lord, how oft shall my brother sin against me, and I forgive him? till seven times? Jesus saith unto him, I say not unto thee, Until seven times: but, Until seventy times seven.*

The Body of Christ has forgotten what the blood of Christ did for us on the Calvary. Yet we have not forgotten what we feel or what we would do to get back at our brothers and sisters in the Body. We are lying, backbiting unloving and hateful. Can't we get along? God is not pleased with us. We continue to be Christians, yet we're still looking for our brother or sister to fall and stay down. The power of forgiveness needs to be surrounded by love and compassion as Christ has shown to us. When will we get it together and show the world that we can forgive and move on in love? When we do, it's going to move us into another realm of God's favor.

Matthew 6:14-15 says, *"For if ye forgive men their trespasses, your heavenly Father will also forgive you: but if ye forgive not men their trespasses, neither will your Father forgive your trespasses."*

Now the scripture says in Galatians 6:1-2, *"Brethren, if a man be overtaken in a fault, ye which are spiritual, restore such an one in the spirit of meekness; considering thyself, lest thou also be tempted. Bear ye one another's burdens, and so fulfil the law of Christ."*

It's time for us to be more sensitive to people and learn to bear their problems and burdens and forgive. We don't have time to judge and point fingers at anyone who falls.

7 Unforgiveness

We should learn from the word. The expression *unforgivness* doesn't really exist in English vocabulary. It is a colloquial term implied to its meaning. It is an attempt to express the opposite of forgiveness.

Unforgiveness brings fear, sickness, doubt and insecurity. It stops the flow of the anointing and favor on your life. Unforgiveness is a sickness and a disease that needs to be healed in the Body of Christ. My recommendation to you is to not associate with anyone who does not forgive, because it can be contagious and poisonous to you when you want the blessing of God in your life.

When there is stiffness, bitterness and disloyalty among the brethren and sisters in Christ, then the Father's heart is saddened. Isaiah 53:3-9 says:

RUDOLPH S. JOHNSON SR.

He is despised and rejected of men; a man of sorrows, and acquainted with grief: and we hid as it were our faces from him; he was despised, and we esteemed him not. Surely he hath borne our griefs and carried our sorrows yet we did esteem him stricken, smitten of God, and afflicted. But he was wounded for our transgressions, he was bruised for our iniquities: the chastisement of our peace was upon him; and with his stripes we are healed. All we like sheep have gone astray; we have turned every one to his own way; and the Lord hath laid on him the iniquity of us all. He was oppressed, and he was afflicted, yet he opened not his mouth: he is brought as a lamb to the slaughter, and as a sheep before her shearers is dumb, so he openeth not his mouth. He was taken from prison and from judgment: and who shall declare his generation? for he was cut off out of the land of the living: for the transgression of my people was he stricken. And he made his grave with the wicked, and with the rich in his death; because he had done no violence, neither was any deceit in his mouth.

Let's remember our Lord's suffering and victory, then we can forgive and be a blessing. Let's love and forgive because it opens a healing path, spiritually mentally physically and financially. The power of forgiveness will allow you to hold your peace as Christ did and gain the victory.

8 Blessing on Forgiveness

Forgiveness is unconditional. You can't earn it. You don't deserve it. You're unable to bargain for it. God gives it to you freely even though it cost him Jesus Christ on the cross.

Forgiveness also doesn't mean you condone. When you forgive, you are not letting others get away with what they did. They may still face punishment. Forgiving them doesn't mean you agree with what they did. Forgiveness doesn't mean the relationship remains the same. It may take some time for you to trust the person again. You may need time to see if his or her repentance is genuine and how the offender works toward offering restitution and rebuilding your trust. You can forgive the offender regardless of his or her attitude. Just as God initiated your forgiveness, you can forgive without requiring the other person to ask for it.

Forgiveness brings you freedom. When you forgive another, you're free to look at the situation in a fresh way and to see how God will make *"all thing work together for the good of those who love God and are called according to His purpose."* (Romans 8:28)

9 Power of Forgiveness

In the power of forgiveness, let's not be selective in whom we forgive. If you cannot put the past behind you and forgive, then your heavenly Father will not forgive you. Let's all operate in the power of forgiveness, because whatever you sow is what you will reap. Let the power of restoration be with you. Forgive, forget and let God heal you.

RUDOLPH S. JOHNSON SR.

10 Will Versus Consciousness

We all have a will and consciousness to forgive when one makes a mistake or sin. In the beginning of his life, Adam was in the dispensation of the innocent. He was without sin. God had provided the most abundant life for him. In Genesis 2, his will took over and he stepped out of perfection. He became aware of what he had done, but God confronted him in Genesis 3:9-10.

When we separate ourselves from the will of God or from the plan he has for us and we do what we want, we get caught naked and ashamed. All because we did not heed the instructions of God. We become sidetracked or distracted by outside sources that do not want us to move into the things of God, but the power of forgiveness gives us all the opportunity to enjoy those blessings. Forgiveness does not excuse us from doing wrong, but understanding it validates the penalty of our sin so we can be in right standing with God. This is what Jesus did for us all. He paid the ultimate sacrifice for us. When the people accused him, he used the power of forgiveness by stating, "Father forgive them, for they know not what they do."

As believers, the Body of Christ, we need to get back to being sensitive and saying, "I forgive them for they know not what they do." When you exercise the power of forgiveness, blessings come to you. It's not that you don't remember the wrong, but you refuse to focus on it. The scripture Proverbs 18:21 says, "Death and life are in the power of the tongue: and they that love it shall eat the fruit thereof." Turn your words into blessing for those who wrong you and for yourself. Fruit will always be ripe in you, and you can watch God heal your spirit, soul and body.

Not forgiving can cause more damage to us—sickness, a lack of communication with God, disloyalty to the things of God, poor finances, overall misery and frustration, and much more. The enemy will play tricks on your mind.

As a body of believers, let's get back to real forgiveness, so people who divorced for no reason can reconcile and show the world real meaning of the power of forgiveness. There is too much flesh on parade and no sincere honesty and forgiveness. Prideful people have caught us by the throat and choked out our love for each other as a reflection of Christ's love for us. He said in his words, forgive. Why can't we do it? Because we have too much of our flesh taking over. As in Galatians 5:19-23, so-called Christians in the church are envious, violent, idolatrous, sinful, hateful and unforgiving. It's time we started being an example of love, joy, peace, gentleness, goodness, faith, meekness and temperance.

The scripture says that when you can't see yourself and point your finger everywhere else, you've become like the Devil, a deceiver and a liar (Galatians 6:1-2) The scripture also says in

Galatians 6:3, *"For if a man think himself to be something, when he is nothing, he deceiveth himself."* When you forgive, love is expressed in a divine way that sees passed the hurt. Let's put the power of forgiveness into action and show the world we can live like Christ would want us to live. He wants us to live a life of abundance, without selfish motives. Paul said, *"Let this mind be in you as also in Christ Jesus."*

I understand pain, but Jesus experienced pain to the fullest and still forgave. John 3:16 says, *"For God so loved the world that he gave His only begotten Son, so that whosoever believeth in him shall not perish but have everlasting life."* Where is your heart when it comes to forgiving?

RUDOLPH S. JOHNSON SR.

11 Give to Forgive

The power of forgiveness will be demonstrated in my life and, as a result, people will be healed and set free to enjoy life the way God intended for it to be in the beginning.

To love is to forgive. It's not that we condone what the person has done to us, but there should be a place in your heart that says, "Love covers a multitude of sins." If we cannot love, we have sinned, and it's just as bad as the other person's sin. Love is the greatest testimony you can give. Love shows no ill feelings, but produces the godly kind of forgiveness that will confuse your enemies.

1 Corinthians 13:4-6 says that charity suffereth long and is kind; that's the power of forgiveness. Charity envieth not, that's the power of forgiveness. Charity vaunteth not itself and is not puffed up, that's the power of forgiveness; does not behave itself unseemly, that's the power of forgiveness; seeketh not her own, that's the power of forgiveness; is not easily provoked, that's

the power of forgiveness; thinketh no evil, that's the power of forgiveness; rejoiceth not in iniquity but in truth, that's the power of forgiveness; beareth all things, that's the power of forgiveness; believeth all things, that's the power of forgiveness; hopeth all things, that's the power of forgivness; endureth all things, that's the power of forgiveness. Where there is love, the power of forgiveness never fails.

Hear the words of Paul in Galatians 2:20 *I am crucified with Christ: nevertheless I live; yet not I, but Christ liveth in me: and the life which I now live in the flesh I live by the faith of the Son of God, who loved me, and gave himself for me.*

The power of Restoration has finally come- to forgive.

ABOUT THE AUTHOR

A postle Rudolph Samuel Johnson, Sr. was born to *Mr. Howard* and *Georgianna Johnson* in 1959, Chestertown, Maryland. Apostle Johnson was very active during his formal years of education. He has performed and sang in theater productions. He recorded with the *Mother C.O,G.I.C. Harvest Choir, Terry L. White, Sr.* as well as *New Generation*. Having sang and performed with the "Greats" of the Gospel Music industry, he recorded and co-produced a CD with his daughters *The Johnson Sisters*.

RUDOLPH S. JOHNSON SR.

The call to preach the word came to Apostle Johnson in 1982. Apostle connected with the *New Pentecostal U.H.C. of America*, under the leadership of *Dr. Louvenia Dickerson* who instructed him through his ministry. Apostle Johnson pursed other studies that would support him in the ministerial work. He received a Bachelor's Degree at the *United Christian College*. In 1999, Apostle answered the clarion call to the Pastoral Ministry establishing the *Restoration World Ministries, Inc.* in Edgewood, Maryland along with his wife, *Prophetess Fern W. Johnson*. He is a man of faith, focus and vision. In June 2008, the Apostle was recognized and awarded for his many years of outstanding and unselfish, dedicated spiritual leadership to the Edgewood Community. He passionately acknowledges, "It's all about helping people."

Two of his favorite scriptures are *St. Matthew 6:33* "*But seek he first kingdom of God and his righteousness and all things will be added unto you.*" *Hebrews 11:1* "*Now faith is in the substance of things hoped for, the evidence of things not seen.*"

This book was published by:
The Glory Cloud publications LLC
P.O. Box 193
Sicklerville, NJ 08081
www.theglorycloudpublications.com
vof1@aol.com

For additional information about us and how to obtain other literature, or how to publish your life story, testimony, miracle report, biography, fiction, or children's story book, please write or email us at the above addresses.

*Psalms 68:11
*Habakkuk 2:3, 4 *2 Corinthians 1-7
*Jude 22

*With our Voice and His Glory, by Faith
Making a Difference in the World*

www.ingramcontent.com/pod-product-compliance
Lightning Source LLC
Chambersburg PA
CBHW070100020526
44112CB00034B/2130